DOCTOR ESPERANTO
AND THE LANGUAGE OF HOPE

Mara Rockliff

ILLUSTRATED BY Zosia Dzierżawska

CANDLEWICK PRESS

Białystok, 1860s

Once there was a town of many languages
but few kind words.

In the town there lived a boy named Leyzer Zamenhof.

He was a gentle boy, and the sharp words cut him like stones.

What made everyone so angry? Leyzer wondered.

Was it because they couldn't understand each other's words?

If they shared a language, he thought, they would understand
each other. If they understood each other, they could live in peace.

But *which* language?

All the people thought that their own language was the best.

Leyzer studied Latin, Greek, and Hebrew. But these old languages were hard to learn.

He decided to make up a
brand-new language of
his own.

He started by inventing very
simple words. But they were
so simple, he got them all
mixed up!

Leyzer tried again. This time, instead of using words that were completely new, he borrowed words from many different languages and tailored them to fit.

tailleur

tailor

TAJLORO

Now anyone could understand at least a little of his language, and a few words were familiar to almost everyone.

kats

Katze

cat

gatto

gato

кот

Kato

Kat

chat

Leyzer's language grew and grew.

But as many words as he made up, he always needed more.

How could he invent a word for everything that anyone would ever want to say? And how could anyone remember all those words?

On the street one day, he saw two signs. Two different words — with the same ending.

What if he made his whole language out of word parts that could fit together many ways?

fiŝeto

fiŝego

fiŝo

fiŝaro

fiŝujo

With these word parts, he could put together enough words to talk about anything in the world!

floreto

floro

florego

floraro

florujo

Leyzer tested his new words over and over. He used them

to write,

to speak,

and to think.

He taught them to the other boys at school.

Finally, he was ready to share his new language with the world.

But his father, so the story goes, said *Nyet.*

Leyzer was going away
to university to be a doctor.
He would need to study hard.
He would have no time to
waste on made-up words.

Sadly, he handed over all his papers.

He watched his father tie them up with string,

put the bundle in a cupboard,

and shut the door.

Leyzer did study. But his heart was with the language
he had left behind.

At last, Leyzer came home. He rushed to the cupboard.

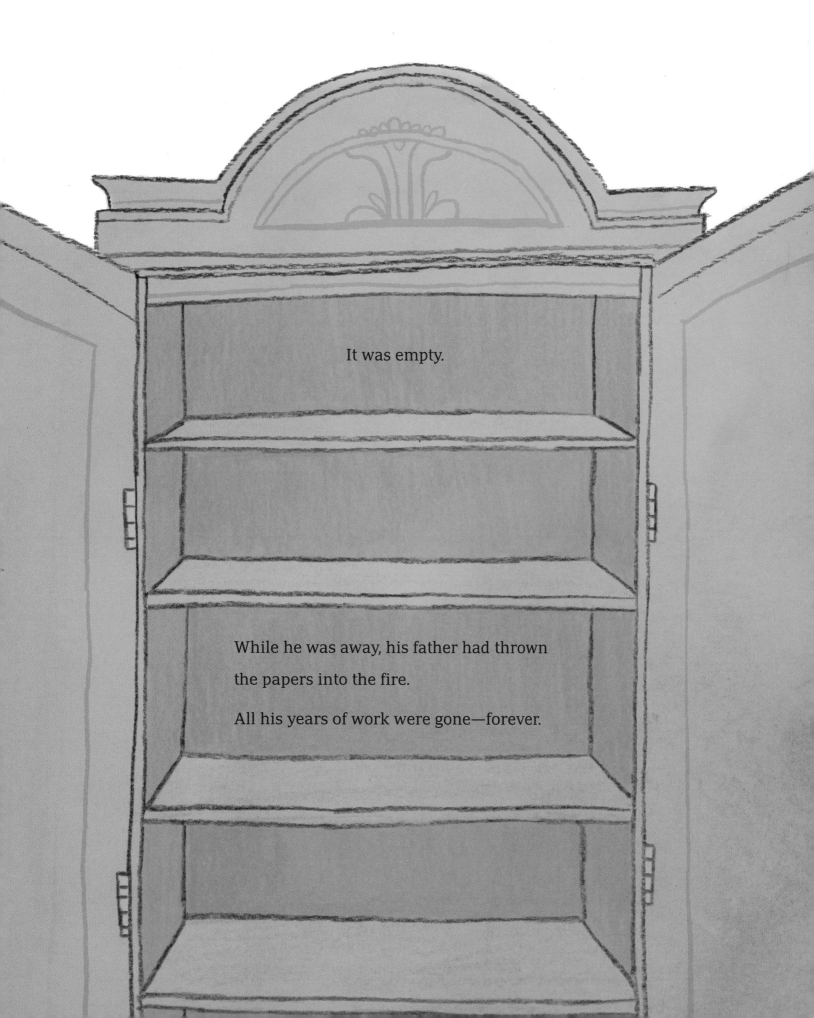

It was empty.

While he was away, his father had thrown
the papers into the fire.

All his years of work were gone—forever.

He began again.

Instead of food, the young doctor bought candles and worked long into the night. This time, his language would be even better, simpler . . . and beautiful enough to tell a young woman named Clara how he felt.

With Clara's help, he put his language into a book.

He didn't sign it *Doctor Zamenhof.*

He signed it *Doctor Esperanto* — "one who hopes."

And he sent it off into the world.

Slowly, the days passed.

Then one letter arrived . . .

and another . . .

and then more and more.

The letters came from near and far, from any place a gentle boy or girl or man or woman dreamed that understanding could bring peace.

They called the language Esperanto, and it gave them hope.

Now the candles burned for both Leyzer and Clara, working long into the night. As many letters as they answered, there were always more.

One day, an invitation came.

A world congress of Esperanto!

While Leyzer's language spread around the world, he and Clara had stayed home. Now they counted out the third-class fare and climbed aboard a train to far-off France.

In Paris, they were whisked off to a party at the Eiffel Tower. Everyone was eager to see "Doctor Esperanto."

But when he stepped onto the congress stage and saw the waiting crowd, he couldn't speak.

So many men and women from so many countries, meeting face-to-face for the first time! What if they couldn't understand each other after all? What if his work had failed?

He gazed out at the people
of the world who had come
so far to share a dream.

And then he found the
words — *his* words.

Mi salutas fratoj

vin, karaj samideanoj, kaj fratinoj el la granda tutmonda homa familio...

They understood!

And when they all rose to their feet and cheered and shouted . . .

Vivu Zamenhof!

he understood them, too.

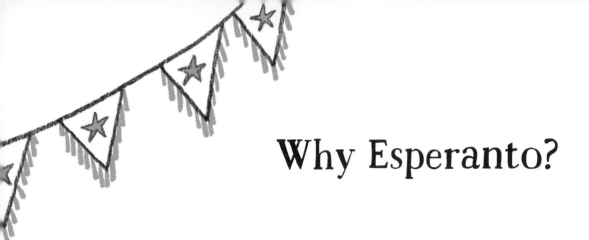

Why Esperanto?

Young Leyzer didn't realize it, but he was not the first to try to create a new world language. In fact, people had been doing it for centuries. The great scientist Isaac Newton had proposed his own universal language more than two hundred years earlier!

When Zamenhof introduced Esperanto to the public in 1887, it was just one of dozens of invented languages making the rounds that year. Yet all the others failed, while Esperanto has survived. Why?

One reason is that, compared to other languages, Esperanto is simple and easy to learn. Nouns always end in *o*. Adjectives end in *a*. And the prefix *mal-* turns a word into its opposite. So if you know that *amiko* means "friend," then you know that "friendly" must be *amika*. And *malamiko* means . . . Can you guess?

Also, in Esperanto, every letter has one sound, and every sound has one letter. This makes Esperanto words easier to spell and pronounce. For instance, *k* is the only letter that makes the "k" sound, and *s* is the only letter that says "s." (Think of a letter in English that can sound like either *k* or *s*.)

If you want to learn Esperanto, there are many resources available online, including the cartoon *Mazi en Gondolando* as well as the popular websites Lernu.net and Duolingo.com. Or you might like to try inventing your own "conlang" (short for "constructed language"), as made-up languages are known today.

Note: Zamenhof made many changes to his language before he finally shared it with the world. To avoid confusion, this book uses Esperanto words as they appeared in his first published books (and continue to be used today).

L. L. Zamenhof (1859–1917) was born in Białystok, a Polish city then under the rule of the Russian Empire. His family called him Leyzer (the Yiddish form of the Biblical name Eliezer), but as a young man he began calling himself Ludovic. Later he was known as Ludwik, with Lejzer or Lazarus often given as his middle name. To speakers of Esperanto, he is simply the one and only Zamenhof.

Life in angry, suspicious Białystok was hard on everyone, but hardest on the Jews, whose religion as well as language set them apart from the Russians, Poles, and Germans. Many years later, Zamenhof would write, "My Jewishness is the main reason why, from my earliest childhood, I gave myself wholly to one overarching idea and dream, that of bringing together in brotherhood all of humanity."

Zamenhof hoped that Esperanto would become a universal language, a "bridge" that would let ordinary people all around the world understand each other and work together for peace. In the years after his first book came out, his dream seemed to be coming true as thousands of enthusiastic followers took up the cause. Esperanto groups formed across Europe and in Africa, Asia, Australia, and America. The new language was praised by many writers, including Leo Tolstoy in Russia, H. G. Wells and J. R. R. Tolkien in Great Britain, and Jules Verne in France.

In 1914, Zamenhof was on his way to the tenth international congress of Esperanto when World War I broke out. Borders slammed shut. As nations took sides, Esperantists found their friends in other countries declared enemies.

Zamenhof didn't live to see peace, but after the war, the Esperanto movement grew. The new League of Nations even considered adopting Esperanto as its official language. Then came World War II. The German dictator Hitler had a special hatred for Esperanto, which he imagined was a Jewish plot to take over the world. Many Esperantists died in Nazi concentration camps, among them Zamenhof's two daughters and his son.

Although Esperanto hasn't become a universal language, it has never disappeared. *The World Almanac* estimates that there are two million Esperanto speakers worldwide. There are Esperanto pop songs, Esperanto magazines and books for kids, and Esperanto videos. (Actor William Shatner starred in the all-Esperanto horror film *Incubus* in 1966, the same year he began playing Captain Kirk on the TV show *Star Trek*.) The language has even been used on *The Simpsons* and in *SpongeBob Comics*, though with some mistakes.

Thanks to the Internet, today it is easier to learn Esperanto and find other speakers than ever before. Speakers can join Esperanto groups for vegetarians, cat lovers, even Scouts. The Universala Kongreso (World Congress of Esperanto) takes place in a different country every year.

Could Esperanto still become a universal language and a bridge to world peace? Some say yes. They hold on to Zamenhof's dream and his motto: *Ni laboru kaj esperu* — "Let us work and hope."

Selected Sources

Boulton, Marjorie. *Zamenhof, Creator of Esperanto.* London: Routledge and Paul, 1960.

Garvía Soto, Roberto. *Esperanto and Its Rivals: The Struggle for an International Language.* Philadelphia: University of Pennsylvania Press, 2015.

Heller, Wendy. *Lidia: The Life of Lidia Zamenhof, Daughter of Esperanto.* Oxford: George Ronald, 1985.

Korzhenkov, Aleksander. *Zamenhof: The Life, Works, and Ideas of the Author of Esperanto.* Translated by Ian M. Richmond. New York: Mondial, 2009.

Maimon, N. Z. *La Kaŝita Vivo de Zamenhof.* Tokyo: Japana Esperanto-Instituto, 1978.

Okrent, Arika. *In the Land of Invented Languages.* New York: Spiegel & Grau, 2009.

Privat, Edmond. *The Life of Zamenhof.* Translated by Ralph Eliott. London: George Allen & Unwin, 1931.

Schor, Esther. *Bridge of Words: Esperanto and the Dream of a Universal Language.* New York: Metropolitan Books, 2015.

Zamenhof, L. L. "Letero al Borovko." *Lingvo Internacia* 6–7 (1896), 115–119.

For all my *karaj samideanoj*, and with
special thanks to István Ertl and Lee Miller.
Koran dankon!
M. R.

For Krzyś—another little boy with big ideas
Z. D.

Text copyright © 2019 by Mara Rockliff
Illustrations copyright © 2019 by Zosia Dzierżawska

Please note that all text in green is in Esperanto.

First edition 2019

Library of Congress Catalog Card Number pending
ISBN 978-0-7636-8915-5

18 19 20 21 22 23 WKT 10 9 8 7 6 5 4 3 2 1

Printed in Shenzhen, Guangdong, China

This book was typeset in Adamant.
The illustrations were done in pencil and ink
and assembled digitally.

Candlewick Press
99 Dover Street
Somerville, Massachusetts 02144

visit us at www.candlewick.com